News of the Changes

NEWS OF THE CHANGES

Bryan Aspden

POETRY WALES PRESS
1984

POETRY WALES PRESS
56 PARCAU AVENUE, BRIDGEND, MID GLAMORGAN

British Library Cataloguing in Publication Data

Aspden, Bryan
    News of the changes
    I. Title
    821'.914   PR6051.S6

ISBN 0-907476-32-5

Cover Illustration : *Study For Quarry Painting* by Peter Prendergast,
from the collection of Eileen and Lewis Allen.
Photograph of drawing by David Garner.

*The publisher acknowledges the financial support of the
Welsh Arts Council.*

Printed in 11pt Baskerville
by
D. Brown & Sons Ltd.,
Bridgend, Mid Glamorgan.

Contents

Acknowledgements

Some of these poems have appeared in the following magazines: *Poetry Wales, Anglo-Welsh Review, New Poetry 8, New Poetry 9, The Poetry Society National Poetry Competition 1980 Prizewinners, Vision On, Y Saeth, An Faner Kernewek.*

i

Julia, Sally a Trefor

News of the Changes

Poems from an Exhibition

1

Chwarel Bethesda—Peter Prendergast

You set your table, bench and drawing board
On the quarry's edge and reach across
With eye and brush, to the far boundary
Between grazing and slate where a farmhouse waits
Above the drop that's swallowed its neighbours,
And a river, guillotined at the workface,
Stepladders down walls, terraces and slabs
Of seabed and estuary banked in stone
Till it reaches the bottom of this inside-out mountain.

No men and no machinery
Are at work in your painting.
There's only the shape they've made
Making a living from slate
By increments of poverty and profit.

Quarry huts, a ruined hawthorn,
The sky's muddy deposits.
Two miles towards the coast,
And out of the picture,
In his cut-out castle among trees,
While a *bwrdd naddu* sits idle in the early Silurian,
George Sholto Douglas Pennant, the owner,
Pours out a glass of Malvern water
And decides not to answer
A letter from the strike committee.

(*bwrdd naddu*—a table where slate is cut)

2

Pentrepella—Kyffin Williams

"nid yw'r graig yn deall Saesneg"
"the rocks don't understand English"- Bethesda saying

Like mud from the beudy
It was not to be brought indoors,
The language farmers used
To talk about bulls
And the birth of calves.
Even your father,
Who only came alive in Welsh,
Had to scrape it off at the doorstep.

Taidi's house—one patched eye,
The other stuck to his telescope—
Was kind to the old words that dawdled
Among thrift, sea campion,
Crempog teas on the farms,
And the Liverpool liners
Washing the Skerries.

But grandfather's—who relished his diary:
"No sermon today, owing to my throat.
The year ends with gloomy prospect,
Owing to Transvaal War"—
Could not stomach
Their half-dressed carollings and chirpings.

School in Trearddur, where the wind slipped its tracts
Under the doors of holiday cottages.
Days on the hills with Bonzo,
Or loafing on Moel y Gest in the sun.
Then the lost years of elocution
At Shrewsbury, four mile runs
And beatings over hot water pipes.

After a botched tonsillectomy
You gave up trying
And drifted as far from words
As your eyes could carry.

Your brother started his career.
They found you articles with Yale and Hardcastle
Off the High Street, Pwllheli.
Land agents of the old school—
Mornings tootling round the estates,
Then a meet with the Border Counties
Or a rough shoot at Nanhoron.
One night in the Anglesey Arms—
You'd been out after duck on the Afon Wen—
A glass of port, Sospan Fach, the Old Grey Mare—
You woke under the snow
On your bedroom floor,
Blood in your mouth, your tongue
A bolster stuffed with pain.

The doctor prescribed
Belladonna, luminal, Irish Moss;
Gave instructions not to use your brain
To excess. You joined the Royal Welsh Fusiliers
As a Second Lieutenant.
The War took you from Pwllheli to Porthmadog,
Across the water to Lurgan
And back, your troops labelled
"Passenger to Pwllheli. I speak no English."
Six months at Maentwrog
Pretending what to do
If the Germans came.
But no dodging the Grand Mal.
"You can't play sir, you're not well,"

As they carried you foaming
From the rugby field.
The medical board found you abnormal
And discharged you to the Slade.

A half world of the Home Guard
And figure drawing.
Three days' teaching a week.
You found it comfy,
Having no talent
And no-one to push you.
On dull evenings,
Drawn by the light behind a roof ridge,
The sheen of wet slate,
You painted your way to Wales.
Even Miss Josling's half-blind cooking—
Bread, butter and marmalade cat hairs,
Your morning kipper grilled
In the News of the World—
Could not stop you following hounds
Down tongues of water
After make-believe otters.

You watched the cliffs break against the sea
At Capel Tywyn,
Slept where the Ynysfor taps
Gushed midnight Guinness.
At Bisham Gardens, N6, you learned
To talk to the rocks
In their own language.

3

Landscape Around December—Ernest Zobole

After five years not painting
On Ynys Môn, you went back to Cwm Rhondda,
Kicked your shoes off on the bedroom lino
And painted the view from the window.

The years peeled off like wallpaper
And the valley arranged itself round your bed.
Slagheaps were knees under the quilt;
Sheep grazed by your left elbow.

And there were presents. Street lights
A row of oranges on your bedside table.
Moon and stars
Shone from their toffee jar.

You made yourself cosy, with a bedwarmer
Filled with cinders from the valley's past.
The chapel on your floor
Glowed like a paraffin heater.

Then, outside your window,
Face blanker than an owl's,
Frost cut through the wires
To deep cold, a dug-out winter.

Headlamps on the valley roads
Lit empty tunnels
And the trees burned
In their moorland bunkers.

When the sky was like dead slag
You took out tubes of ochre,
Cadmium red,
The undepleted ore

And painted all you could remember,
All that was there,
Painted this birth
"Landscape around December."

Bedtime

"Draw a picture of soldiers going boom-boom
In a war-war. Colour in their legs and their armour."
He does the gunfire, a red spider
Crawling from the barrel of a rifle,
While I'm detailed to do tanks and aeroplanes
And put in their country (RAF rondels
Or a black cross) over a Maginot line
Tunnelled like a Gruyère, with lifts, ladders,
And bunks full of soldiers sleeping in their tin hats.
It takes me a long way back, to the nights
When I drew them behind the blackout
And the sky was jigsawed by searchlights
And shrapnel fell, to be picked up like conkers
In the morning on the way to school;
Or the days when the warning went before hometime
And we sat in the shelter with our biscuits,
Our tin of cocoa, our monster-making gasmasks.
He adds felt-tip fire to the wings of a plane.
Smoke covers half his computer paper sky.
"Do those things you had instead of sparklers.
You know, inside a room, in a war."
We huddle in bed together, waiting for the all clear,
Drawing indoor fireworks: Bengal Lights,
Invisible writing, a paper bag balloon, its tray of fire.

Postcards from Anne

The postcards come, with leopards, elephants,
Stamped in Bombay or Kenya, somewhere in the States,
To print their gloss of sunlight on the morning mat
And face us, over our wholemeal wheatflakes,
With adverts of adventure—eyes and teeth,
A dirt path loping off into the bush; third
Or new world cities; and she's there, walking
Their pavements, lecturing, listening. We try
To take them in; but we live here, among our cats
And hens. India fades, its myriads and tongues,
Compared with learning Welsh, or breast stroke,
Or meeting Andrea in the swimmimg pool.
Sellotaped to the wall, postcards have their season
Till damp or drought unstick them and they fall,
Curling and brown, to winter on the floor.

Dewi Emrys

I had a career. Respectability
Fed me. I preached, received a stipend;
Advised if not shepherded my flock;
Until a different angel took me by the hand.
Words bettered me; I fled. Echoing
Sion Pywel, who washed his shirt by lying
In a stream, I swapped my Presbytery
For the ditch. No roof but rain, newspaper
For quilt and groundsheet; and yet
The world, though it ceased paying, still praised.
Chaired or crowned at each Eisteddfod, I might have turned
Presentable again, but I was seized
And shaken. One dizzying vision burned
Into my brain, above the precipice.

The cleft in stormlight like a hanging rope
Went down two hundred feet into Pwllderi
The night I lowered myself to wreckers' cove
In mind, for none had stepped there but the heron,
Seal, stilt-legged seabirds and Dai Becca.
Mackerel glitter lit the water, then I saw
Sailor's corpse still beckoning turn on the tide;
Gone like a lantern. Never a drop
Of decency's watered spirits touched my lips
Since then. From Dyfed speech I made this marvel,
My poem 'Pwllderi'. I, Dewi Emrys,
An old man, a ruin of drink and dandruff
Still after the girls, doddering
Into glory. The good Lord keep your soul.

Ludlow

Out of Wales and away
From the holiday traffic
We come to a countryside
Not drowsy, quite,

But scratching its head
For something it can't remember:
"Waen, Nant yr—, Weston Rhyn,
The Long Mynd, Leintwardine—"

The last Welsh placenames
Caught by the prickles
Of their new accent
And carried like burrs on a sheep's back

Over these hills where Housman brewed
For our refreshment his nettle beer:
"In my heart it has not died,
The war that sleeps on Severn side—"

Church Stretton, self-satisfied
As a training camp for officers
Behind the lines, greets us
With a snappy salute of road signs.

Picnic lunch, then Ludlow
Where history's a secondhand bookshop
Opening late in the afternoon
And knocking off 50p to a cautious buyer.

Anne and Richard, here from Dorset,
Quiz the wormy tables,
The chessboard walls that prop each other up
With the air of a comedown class

Who are making a packet from trade
And keeping a bottle in the cashdrawer.
In an automatic cafe we exchange Sally
For a Pride of India and a Cotoneaster.

Talk about our holiday in the Gaeltacht
Till Anne outbids us
With her round the world cruise
Paid for by the Moonies;

Then kisses, see you in a week,
And we drive off down the Ice Age valley
Where brachiopod and trilobite,
Disturbed in their siltstone beds,

Wake in the veins of snails
And get up as shells again.
At Glyndwr a moraine of cars
Frets at a landslide;

Then it's loosed
And we flow towards the coast
And home,
Three of us where there were four.

The journey thrums in our ears
And our skin crawls
As if touched by pumice
Or a dry sponge.

Nant Honddu

(for David Jones)

A grail of gorse; basketwork hedges
Threaded with birds. It's the end of March;
Spring still an outline map. These windflowers
And a purse of woodsorrel all that's filled in—

Two memories merging from the same month
Ten years apart, and at different ends of the path
That crosses your land and marks its eastern border.
When you were here you painted two black ponies

Grazing in a cup of the hills; a wattle fence;
Lopped ash and oak; a coverlet of fields;
Forestry rising to the shaved head of the moor—
A land man had neighboured long enough

To turn its grudge to giving—though the gifts
Weren't even-handed, nor was the taking.
You hankered for its comfort, grown up away.
After the first war came here to paint, to study, to recover.

You painted the river coming from Penny Beacon
Or Hay Bluff, past Capel-y-Ffin, Pont-y-Wyrlod
To Garn Farm, Dôl Alice, Crucorney
Where three centuries of change have got their tongues

Round the place names, and Englished but not misplaced them.
Ten years ago I drove the Austin Cambridge
By the side of Nant Honddu, parked where the sign
Pointed a peglegged walker over Hatterall Hill

Away from Wales, to Hereford cattle and apples.
Today in the wind's gap above Bodfari I watch
Sheep, a sheepdog, two ponies; try to learn
Like you "the creatureliness of things"; find
Some kindly forms, words that would heal the hurt
Of this land with its boundary in its heart.

Evacuees

A scarf of Mersey fog round their throats,
They scuffed the pavements
For threepenny bits the sun might have left
As it looked at them sideways
Before moving on. Autumn
Poured out a homebrew of sooty rain
Almost the same as where they came from.
They pecked between our railings,
Grubbed through our mash of gardens
And gathered in the playground
Chattering like the last leaves of a hedge.

"Lend us a tanner till tomorrow—"
Their October subsong.
In the morning their desks were empty.
They were found to have flown
To their bombed and treeless streets,
To those who might understand
Why sparrows would migrate.

Schön Rosmarin

You tried to hide them from me, the Picture Post
Photographs from the camps where men
Thinned to their own X-rays, their flesh
Having made it across the wire.
Crooks, queers, subversives, those
Patched by a rag star and cattle-trucked
Across Europe—you put them
Under "Schön Rosmarin" in the piano stool.

They stayed there for a quarter century.
One day, visiting, you fell down
The Charnwood steps. The deep cut hardly bled.
How long the snow had lain, beneath rouged cheeks,
We couldn't guess; not even when, in bed
For eighteen months, you would pretend
To eat until your failed breath told
The three stone secret under the sheets.

Llydaw

. . . a part of memory's coastline
Where gannets or terns
Whiten the bay
And the wind spits white foam off the waves;

Nobody comes but a fisherman
Saying it is going to rain
In a voice so soft
It hardly touches the silence.

His eyes with that courtesy
That offers itself but does not insist,
He balances on the road's edge,
Knowing how easily he might capsize on land,

Then walks to where his boat
Is drawn on the shingle,
Watches the air for a while,
Nods and goes home;

Almost, it might be thought,
That he had not been there,
Except that his absence
Still quietly holds the scene.

Today

We visit Prestatyn. From limestone hill
Look down, like kestrels, on the holiday
Seaside town. This is called Fish Mountain,
High land where once the ocean had its way.
Here one inch deep is fathoms of grey bone,
A hardened sea where skeleton and shell
Swim in the undercurrents of the hill
And fish have surfaced from the stone.
Quarry scree fans to an estuary.
We settle beside it, start our picnic.
Curled like a question mark a cat suggests
Another world of time where hardness
Melts and flows, no barrier's placed between
Stone and sea, stillness and motion.

On this quarry floor, hacked from the ocean,
Buddleia, Old Man's Beard, blue butterflies
Scent and stain, inscribe the air, bright living
Offsets of a fossiled shore. These are death's
Afterthoughts the cat from its bramble
Tunnel understands, for it has tested
With micro-sensitive paws both worlds
That merge, are one, and then are parted.
Here too is where division's signposted:
"Llwybr Clawdd Offa. Offa's Dyke Path";
With a concrete acorn underneath.
Stone in a waterdrop suspended falls.
I watch and wonder what language will be
Spoken here when the stone has turned to sea.

News of the Changes

He wears Clarks Movers, his new shoes,
And carries papers to the typing pool,
The section's outmost chamber where
They press him for juice from the centre.
He tells them Colin's here and has made
A Maginot Line of cabinets and trays;
That Maureen's firm and will not move to Legal;
That John Morris the translator
Has changed rooms and taken his kettle.
Sweetened with news they loose him and he goes
Back to his office, where Llew's arrived to toy
With screens and arrows, bilingual signs—all the godwottery
Of order; until the morning's leaked away, and it's time
For sandwiches, and then his lunch hour walk.

He goes past the Pier Pavilion,
The Grand Hotel, The Pier, Happy Valley,
Alex Munro's open-air follies,
The Druids' Circle, the cable car station,
Queen Victoria in her stone pagoda,
Alice, and the White Rabbit, down the steps
To the beach. The tide's coming in. An oystercatcher
Scissors at its edge, and turnstones
Are dabbling their toes in its paper doilies.
As the rocks go under, barnacles
Unbuckle their shells and feed with their feet.
The waves revise their tenses, their soft mutations:
"Ll—", they say coming in; "L—",going out.

At two o'clock he returns to the Town Hall,
To his desk, and the silt of years clogging his in-tray;
Minutes of sub-committees; dictionaries, forms;
Sonnets; Catalan Grammar; *The Way to Write*.

He's done well from the changes. Is a senior fish
In the local government swim. Others
Are left dry and they complain—
Why should they work the word processor,
Learn floppy discs and software on MO1?
These bubbles of displacement stir
The shallows of the afternoon. He's had enough.
He clocks out early, escapes into the car park.
The Mini that he slipped a disc in's gone.
He drives home in the Mazda past Ffon Tom.

Water Colours

In the old reading room, where the unemployed
Angled like herons over the job columns
For a trout from that sluggish stream,
And the afternoon drunks snoozed
Over 'Y Faner' and 'The Church Times',
There's an exhibition this week: Water Colours
By Local Artists. Each frame's enclosed
A babble of green fields in rural Wales
Where all roads are lanes, hedges layered or grown
Into a cave of leaves. There's no barbed wire;
No bedstead mending a gap in the stone wall.
No traffic; no tourists. Almost, it seems,
No people—except that the farms are cared for
And the cottages have just been whitewashed.

Walking deeper in water colour land
We mark these occupations: a tractor,
Driven by two brush strokes of tweed
And the smudge of a cap, ploughing a field.
A farmer herding sheep with two dogs, no landrover.
In late summer a post van parks by the farmyard.
Its scarlet complements the overflow
Of green. Then heat-hazy hills; the first cornet notes
Of the September birch trees, tuning up
For the tone poem, 'Autumn Tints'.
And now in this room it's winter. White swathes
Cumber the fields and we are cold,
In a land without a language, whose troubles lie
Outside the frame with its red circle "sold".

Leaving

He's leaving tomorrow, and must hand over
His canister of marker pens and biros,
His plastic bag of stamps marked URGENT,
The byelaws that he'd have us know he'd drafted,
The Mayor's chain, the ceremonial cushion;
The visitor's book signed by the Queen,
Photographs of the old Town Council days;
The Conwy Harbour Order. 'Lumley's Public Health'—
To those who will forget their use, and care,
Quicker than tadpoles lose their tails. His thumbs
Are plump with arthritis, and weak, but how
Can he let go, just like that, forty years
Of Minuting? Yet he goes, and someone from Hiraethog
Cleans his nest of drawers from the room.

Lumb Bank

It's settled. The Special Personnel Agenda's
Posted, and Catrin will go to the Brickworks
Site Inspection. Leave card, flexitime
Credit form are filled in. I've packed
Craig Raine's poems, Don Quijote,
Warm clothes for the Pennines. On Monday
I catch the train towards the gritstone hills
Where poetry first lodged in my mind,
A sycamore key in a backyard crack
Whose sapling shoves past the sooty privy
After the light. Bark scuffed by boots,
Twigs jiggered by penknives, it's got a hope.
Yet it's still there. Grubbed up, the yard resurfaced,
Shoots from bits of roots squeeze through the tarmac.

The train chunners out of the Junction
And I lean back, listening to the gossip
Of rails and stations—who's still here,
What's going now, what used to be—
Nodded over fences in out of work corners of towns.
A field that can't afford a new coat talks to itself
While it grazes car hulks, a donkey, backstreet sheep.
Newton-le-Willows, Manchester, an embankment
Where an escaped inmate of the Corporation Park,
A rhododendron with green fingers
And amethyst signet rings, hobnobs
With moorland bilberry and heather. I remember
How, on summer picnics, sandstone
Slipped away, with a gritty whisper, under my thumb.

Hebden Bridge, once a wool town and a cotton town,
Where two rivers that used to work for their living
Meet for a natter. Its factory chimneys
Have given up smoking. Its stones
Have lost their grime and wear instead
A sooty lichen. I lug my hold-all
From the station, through the streets,
Into the snackbar; write postcards home
"Annwyl Sally, annwyl Trefor... " I tell them
I'm here and the weather's cloudy; then catch the bus
Through Heptonstall to Lumb Bank
And wait by the water tower, while a draught
From the West Riding's cold furnace
Rakes off the journey's dross, and rakes the grass.

The wind, the water tower, the flattened grass,
The stone walls with their halfmoon copings
Tag my memory. I'm on, chasing through the playground;
Then home, eight year old knees stiffened to sticks
From the stone floor. The next participant
Of the course arrives and we walk down
To the former millowner's house, now
A writing centre where two poets will try
By sleight of hand or by osmosis
To get across some knack of their own
Spinning or weaving. An evening meal,
The house rules for conviviality; the pub
Till closing time, whisky till three. The dawn chorus
At Lumb Bank, and the wren with its North Country accent.

Coffee, breakfast, the first tutorial,
And then a walk. Slack, Jack's Bridge,
Blackshaw Head; Cally Hall Farm—slabs
Not slates for roofs: freedom here is staying put
In the wind. Broadbacked moortops;
Curlew, peewit, a highrise lark;
A commonwealth of blackfaced sheep.
A good view of the Yorkshire bathing belle,
The water rat, in its black swimsuit
Wobbling out of Colden Brook. The Pennine Way,
With its worn-out acorn, hitches through a stile.
"When the factory chimneys were pouring smoke,"
Two farmers tell me. "We were right and got on.
Visitors hardly bring a penny."

A stile here is where walls hutch up to each other
And leave enough room for your knees
But not sheep's or cows', to get through.
In the afternoon we walk to Hardcastle Crags.
Malcolm talks of the technique he'd need
To write a perfect poem, and would he even then?
He's very sad. He puts his head to the ground
And listens to the clatter that ants make
As they hump their bed and breakfast over the cobbles
To their workhouse of heather bells and grass stalks.
He stands up, sees a zepedee of wire
And a rusty fleece on a fence, but won't be convinced
Words can gather such tangles. We sit by the mill lake,
Munching chocolate, and talk about technique.

Five days, five late nights later, writing
Comes to a stop, in sheds of almost sleep.
It's time for home and jobs, fitting poetry
In the cracks of living. We drift from each other
To cars, to the station. The journey back draws in
Histories, longings. Chester walls an hourglass
Telling the time since the Romans. The limestone
Outcrop, where Offa's Dyke begins. And I'm there,
Fielding knowledge, questions, news: astronauts
Are weightless and must wash inside a drum.
Are islands fastened underneath, or floating
On the sea? Julia has coped with Grandpa's
Burning bedclothes. The ordinary world
Clacks back and to on its loom.

Which We Are

Charnwood, standing with its tin hat on
Among a Home Guard of gooseberry prickles
And blackcurrants loaded with the dud grenades
Of big bud, remembered its war service
On Kinmel Camp and squinted as it spied
Two strangers from its uncurtained windows.
When we moved in, the garden followed us
Through the door—not that we knew one from the other
Where the honeysuckle wangled its way
Under the wallpaper, and bats whittled at the evening
Inside the walls, till their fur cooled
And they poured themselves into the dusk.
Through the windows, in spring, we heard
A raven getting stuck on its first verb.

Gwynt-y-Mynydd creaks like its own footsteps
On the stairs. Rain taps the roof.
We live inside a drum and we are part
Of the music that we're listening to.
Under the clouded pewter of the winter skies
The mountain comes closer, pushing
Humped fields with their boulder scree of sheep.
When it's almost dark Trefor has a choice
Of Mad Dan Dado with his matchstick spaceship
Or Un Llygoden Fach waving his cutlass
Over a translated Armada. Five more minutes
One for each year, then it's ''amser''. He concentrates
On wasting nothing. ''Tell me a story,'' he asks.
''Tell it in Welsh or English, which we are.''

Sand Spurrey

It seemed to have strayed
Almost as far as we had,
This castaway beach
On the heather moor.
Overhead a peewit shook
Its tumbler of feathers
And called our eyes
From its nest.

We might have made
For the hills of Hiraethog
Whose heads were above water,
Or followed the road
To Pentrellyncymer,
When we spotted,
On a tracing of silica
In the cracked peat
Of an old cutting
This dayglow marker
"You are here."

Butterwort

Among the ooze and drip
Where hillside and waterfall
Are synonymous
And a foot sunk
Shin deep is safer
Than one planted
On the green slime of rock
The elegance of this velvet hat
On its stand (with the posy of miniature daffodils
In its crown)
Surprises and attracts
In the dark window
A lost bee might stumble on.

Stonecrop

Below a row of houses
Thatched with stars
The quarry path trudging off

Without a word
From lungs that test
The surgeon's knife

In stone fields
The chough reaps
With its red sickle

There's a small bitter flower
On a stem of wire
Beaded with pebbles

That has no need to migrate
Having learned to cadge
A drink from slate.

Sundew

Face poking
Through old curtains of moss
What can it offer
Living alone in the dark
In the backlands
Between sky and peat
On a broth of peatwater?

Instead of the sun
A golden handshake—
These sovereigns of glue.
It licks the flies
From sticky fingers.

Nettle

When the mist clears
No angel takes the fugitives
From the leafless forest
Under its wing.

This greygreen mullah
With the tassel beard
And the white hairs
Hooking from his skin

Rises from his mattress
And offers

To the robin in its kettle
To the wren dossing among cans
To the gormless hedgehog
To the shrew ringing its bell as it goes

To the naked slug and the snail
In its slow cart

The protectorate
Of his poisoned tongue.

Daffodils, Windflowers

The wind levelled at us over the hedge
And loosed its buckshot of thorns
To chase us from the field where March lambs
Were munching the shivery grass.
We'd been trying to find our way
Into Cefn Coed, a wood that had grown
On one of those backbones of shale
The Ice Age had scraped clean, catching the soil
In cupped hands in between.

                  The path
Had a signpost where it left the road
But then it branched, branched again
And some lengths petered out in cattle pools,
While others were stopped with wire. The one we took,
Worn to flaky rock, brought us up grey steps
To a schoolroom of backward trees,
Handicapped by their birth on stone
And the dark roof they grew under.
That someone had cut them to foot-high stumps
Had done nothing to solve their overcrowding.
Each stump had set four or five saplings
With bony arms and scabbed knees,
The botched coppice of a tenant farmer
Wearing the soil to its last stitch
And getting by till postwar wages
Made off with his cheap labour,
And the land pottered on by itself.

A wire fence hung from the brambles
On the ridgetop. It had bagged enough leafmould
For a seed to uncurl in, then lizard into a crack
Till its roots found substance in the rock
And grew to the size trees can expect
Who are closetted with their own shadow.

One silver birch had died, but not fallen,
In the arms of a holly bush, the corpse of a knight
Kept up by his armour, and no-one could tell
Which feet were dead and which were iron.

The path went off downhill and came
To where a mixed herd of Austin 7s,
Ford pickups and a guernsey-coloured Volkswagen
Were grazing a pasture of dock and bracken,
Their russet number plates and dappled bumpers
Another example of the way
Our rural economy mooches forward
With the times. One had rolled onto its back
And lay hardly moving. Another swayed
Kneedeep in nettles, while briars
Switched its side. We could have stayed admiring
But the March cold chivvied us back to the car,
Crisps, ham rolls and coffee. A closed quiet,
Hedge rattle and lamb bleat shut out.
Just our own munching as we noticed
Daffodils huddled in a farm drive
And windflowers sheltering in a wood
That like ourselves had taken the first step
Into the spring's wintry sunshine.

That night on the box, two refugees
Who'd escaped from the camp
Where the war's afterthoughts had penned them
And landed on this farm in mid Wales.
Just their initials were given, no names,
In case the barbed wire should stretch
To the damp acres that had become
Not home but a place where their homelessness
Could bring its muck indoors
And ease its blisters by the fire.

They'd no ambition for crops or cattle
And had never raised them before.
It was their luck that the farm had fallen
Into the state of neglect
Their passports would admit them to
And their pockets could afford.
Their neighbours hardly knew them
Though they picked up the clues—
The milk churn waiting on the railway sleeper,
A wild hedge lying down with its ears back,
Pasture drains singing with a clear throat—
That showed they were, if not reclaiming the land,
Spiriting a living from its dereliction
And making these stained pages
Of the green book of Carmarthenshire
Readable again. The grocer's van,
Steaming up the lane once a month,
Left tins of Marie Biscuits, Four Square Yellow,
And weighed-out packets of roasted coffee.

The farmhouse with its tousled roof
And shabby walls becomes them.
Like the brown tidemark
In their coffee cups, and the grey vests
And amorphous underpants they go to bed in,
It wears the roughcast of their lives.
K kneels to say his prayers
Beneath the ikon and the cross that hang
Among the flakes of cobwebbed plaster.
Then his fingers work
Along their nightly page of Bible,
Patient as the rain that shares his bedroom
And patters by his side
As he climbs between the sheets.

Leaning back on the pillow he feels
For the cord he's fitted through the wall. One tug.
Outside, gutter pulls away from gutter.
The waterwheel slows. The dynamo slows.
The light goes slowly out.

On a hard day in Spring
The wheel of a loaded barrow
Goes against the trenched mud
In the farmyard.
It sticks halfway up a ridge
And can't get over. Slips back
And tries again
From a starting pad of glue. The camera
Doesn't show who's pushing, but we know.
It's given us already
The wings of W's moustache
Lifted in flight as his cracked cheeks
Give rise to a student song.
"Gaudeamus igitur," he crows,
Tipsy with remembered wine.
K on the other hand,
Dunking his trowel in cement, fudging
Slates from the pigsty into the roof,
And digging up the last of the cesspool,
Is pure mudman.

Prompted by his secondhand spectacles
W takes out his English
And exercises it across the kitchen table.
"The train will be ... minutes ... hours
(And a half) late. I would like a ticket
To Birmingham / London / the Isle of Man.
Is this the platform for the five seventeen?"

Loosed like pigeons from his phrasebook.
K has to sweat it out with words.
He hammers them down the telephone
Into the Cardiff operator. Welsh placenames
Spelled with a Slavonic alphabet;
Baltic rivers draining from his forehead
Into the Bristol Channel.

One day the priest for exiles, who never
Says where he's been or where he's going,
But knows the currents
Messages elver through
From one Europe to the next,
Brings news of K's son, who's getting married.
The photographs come—
Grandchildren, feastdays, first communion—
Of a family he'll never meet.
"Life is troubles," he comes out with,
Standing above the boundary stream.
"Without them it would be nice
But it wouldn't be life."
He may or may not notice the daffodil
Holding its crucifix in the Easter wind,
And the windflowers dressed in white
Lowering their heads. He takes in
Where the path has slipped down the bank
That will need a day's work to shore up again.